The Ali Abbasi Joke book 2

The Ali Abbasi Joke book 2

foreword by
Ford Kiernan
and Greg Hemphill

www.vitalspark.co.uk

The Vital Spark is an imprint of
Neil Wilson Publishing
303a The Pentagon Centre
36 Washington Street
GLASGOW
G3 8AZ
Tel: 0141-221-1117
Fax: 0141-221-5363
E-mail: info@nwp.sol.co.uk
www.vitalspark.co.uk

A catalogue record for this book is available
from the British Library.

ISBN 1-903238-34-X
Typeset in Ellington

Printed by WS Bookwell

Contents

Acknowledgements

ANOTHER YEAR, another book and what good fun it's been putting this one together. Being based in Scotland is the ideal place to have a laugh. We have a great sense of humour and an ability to laugh at each other that many may find slightly too close to the bone.

It was impossible to include all the jokes and gags I've collected this past year: after all, this is a family book! I'm hoping once again that no individuals or specific groups of people take any of the jokes personally. There were a whole load of people who helped me, mostly people I've never met. Those I actually do know include: John Beattie, Jack MacConnell, Frank Mungall, Alan McPhee, Stewart Prodger at www.mirth.co.uk, Ken Anton, Roshan Abbasi, John Malcolm (Glasgow taxi driver), Jim Reid, Giles (barman in Hubbard's public house in Glasgow) and Frank Smith.

My special thanks go to Ford Kiernan and Greg Hemphill for writing the foreword. And thanks also to the readers of the *Sunday Post* who sent in loads of gags for inclusion in this book.

Hope you enjoy this one as much as the last ...

Ali Abbasi

Foreword by
Ford Kiernan and Greg Hemphill

ALI ABBASI. The traffic guy on the radio who tells jokes. Every time we meet Ali in the corridors of the BBC his wee face lights up, and he raises his hand to stop you. A sure sign that you are about to receive a joke. The kind of joke that does exactly what it says on the tin. A bog standard chuckle. A street joke. The kinda gag your father would tell you. A joke you wouldn't be ashamed to pass on as your own. But let's get one thing straight right away. Seventy-five per cent of Ali's jokes are mince. Rotten. Toe curlingly bad. Not only that, but it's the way he tells them. Bad timing, emphasis in the wrong parts leaving both parties feeling awkward at the end. The other twenty-five per cent are gold, baby. Pure gold. Beautifully delivered. Excellently timed, eye-wateringly funny. Admittedly, we have never been party to the golden twenty-five per cent but we have heard talk.

Which is why it's always a pleasure to see Ali scurry towards you of a morning. Maybe, just maybe, this time, this is gonna be the one. That's the great thing about his jokes. At the beginning, they hold so much promise. They're all great. That feeling of expectation. Maybe this will be the ultimate joke. Joke Nirvana. Dear God, let Ali be in his zone today. Not more mince, please. We couldn't handle any more ducks inside biscuit tins, barmen wiping their bars with budgies, frogs with motorcycles, men with alcoholic mice in their top pockets. Crab paste from Boots. C'mon, Ali. Go for it. Pull out the stopper and tell us a whopper!

We wish you a tear of joy, a tickled rib and maybe if you're lucky, a map of China on the front of yer troosers.

Enjoy!
Ford and Greg

Ethnic, Cultural (and Irish!)

THIS IRISH guy goes into a bar in the Greek Islands. Sinead, an Irish girl who is working behind the bar, takes his order and notices his Irish accent. Over the course of the night they talk quite a bit. At the end of the night he asks her if she wants to sleep with him. Although she is attracted to him she says no. He then offers to pay her £100 for the deed. Sinead is travelling the world and because she is strapped for cash she agrees.

The next night the same guy turns up again and after showing her plenty of attention throughout the night he asks if she will sleep with him again for £100. She figures in for a penny in for a pound – and she'd had a great time the previous night – so she agrees. This goes on for five nights. On the sixth night the guy comes into the bar, but this time he orders a beer and just goes and sits in the corner. Sinead is disappointed and thinks that maybe she should pay him more attention. She goes over and sits next to him. She asks him where he is from and he tells her Cork.

'Wow, so am I,' she says. 'What part of Cork?'

'Montenotte,' he says.

'Well Holy God! That's amazing,' she says. 'So am I – what street?' And so he names the street.

'This is unbelievable,' she says, 'what number?'

'Number 20,' he says. The girl's astonishment knows no bounds and she is gob-smacked.

'You are not going to believe this,' she says, 'My parents live in number 22!'

'I know,' he says. 'Your da gave me 500 quid to give you!'

AN ENGLISHMAN, an Irishman and a Scotsman are all sent to hell. The devil tells them that before they are sent into the bowels of hell and sentenced to eternal damnation, that they'll have to receive their punishment first. They are each to receive 500 lashes from Satan's fiery whip but they're each allowed one request.

The Scotsman says, 'I'll go first. I want to get it over with.'

To which Satan replies; 'What is your one request then?'

'I want a pillow strapped to my back.'

So the devil gets him a pillow and gives him his 500 lashes. The Scotsman crawls away in agony.

Next the Englishman, feeling a bit smug says 'I'll go next, but I want five fireproof mattresses strapped to my back!'

The devil, disgusted, has to grant his request. Five hundred lashes later the Englishman laughs and stands aside to watch the Irishman receive his punishment.

'Sooooo,' says Satan, 'what do you want then? Ten fireproof mattresses I suppose?'

'No, I want you to strip that English idiot naked and strap him to my back!'

WHAT DO you call an Egyptian taxi driver ?

Toot an cumoot!

WHAT DO you call a Japanese car thief?

Tommy Tookamotah!

THE BARMAN is washing his glasses when an elderly Irishman comes in. With great difficulty, the Irishman hoists his bad leg over the barstool, pulls himself up painfully, and asks for a sip of Irish whiskey. The Irishman looks down to the end of the bar and says, 'Is that Jesus down there?' The barman nods, so the Irishman asks him to give Jesus an Irish whiskey too.

The next patron to come in is an ailing Italian with a hunched back, moving very slowly. He shuffles up to the barstool and asks for a glass of Chianti. He, too, looks down the bar and asks if it's Jesus. The barman nods, so the Italian asks for glass of Chianti for Him as well.

The third patron to enter the bar is a Greenockian, who swaggers into the bar and yells, 'Barman, set me up a Buckfast! Haw, is that God's Boy down there?' The barman nods, so the Greenockian asks him to give Jesus a Buckie.

As Jesus gets up to leave, he walks over to the Irishman, touches him and says, 'For your kindness, you are healed!' The Irishman feels the strength come back to his leg, so he gets up and dances a jig out the door. Jesus then touches the Italian and says, 'For your kindness, you are healed!' The Italian feels his back straighten, and he raises his hands above his head and does a back-flip out of the door.

Then Jesus walks toward the Greenockian, but the Greenockian jumps back, shouting, 'Don't touch me! I'm claiming disability!'

A LINGUISTICS professor is telling his class: 'In English, a double negative forms a positive. In some languages, though, such as Russian, a double negative is still a negative. However, there is no language where a double positive can form a negative.'

Then a lone Scottish voice pipes up from the back: 'Aye, right.'

TONTO AND his mate the Lone Ranger are astride their trusty steeds, making steady progress over the plain, when they draw up beside a body of water to slake their thirsts.

Tonto dismounts, laying his ear close to the ground to try and hear if anything is approaching. 'Buffalo come!' he says on rising.

'Well, I gotta hand it to you! You Indians just seem to know everything, but tell me, how do you know they are buffalo?' asks the Lone Ranger.

Wiping the side of his head Tonto says, 'Face sticky.'

A SCOTSMAN was stuck in a cell with a deadly snake, a tiger and an Englishman. In his revolver he had two bullets. What do you think he did?

He shot the Englishman with the first bullet, then shot him again with the second one just to make sure.

A YOUNG woman in Chicago had twin boys that she gave up for adoption. One was adopted by a couple in Spain, and was called Juan. The other one was adopted by a couple in Egypt, he was called Amall. Many years later Juan finds his birth mother, and sends his picture to her. She's very happy, at first, but then starts feeling a little sad.

Her husband asks, 'What's wrong?'

She said, 'I wish I also had a picture of Amall.'

The husband says, 'But they are twins ... if you've seen Juan, you've seen Amall.'

WHEN CHARLES de Gaulle decided to retire from public life, the British ambassador and his wife threw a gala dinner party in his honour. At the dinner table the ambassador's wife was talking with Madame de Gaulle. 'Your husband has been such a prominent public figure, such a presence on the French and international scene for so many years! How quiet retirement will seem in comparison. What are you most looking forward to in these retirement years?'

'A penis,' replied Madame de Gaulle.

A huge hush fell over the table. Everyone heard her answer ... and no one knew what to say next.

Le Grand Charles leaned over to his wife and said, 'Ma cherie, I believe ze English pronounce zat word, 'appiness!'

A MEXICAN gentleman goes in to apply for a job at the local fast food restaurant and asks to speak to the manager. The manager invites him into his office and tells him, 'There isn't much required for the job but you must be fluent in English.' The Mexican replies, 'Really, well that is not a problem.' The manager responds, 'Can you prove your fluency by using pink, yellow, green and statue in a sentence?' The Mexican thinks for a bit and says, 'Okay, here is a little story. One time I was sitting at home waiting for my friend to call. The phone went green, green so I pink it up and said yellow, Rodriguez is statue?'

DID YOU hear about the Englishman who locked his keys in his car?
It took him an hour and a half to get his family out.

HOW DOES every ethnic joke start?
By looking over your shoulder.

Sex and Marriage

AN AMERICAN man and a Swiss man sit next to a Scotsman on an overseas flight. After a few cocktails, the men begin discussing their private lives.

'Last night, I made love to my wife four times,' the American brags, 'and this morning she made me a special breakfast of cold cereal and scrambled eggs and told me how much she adored me.'

'Ah, last night I made love to my wife six times,' the Swiss responds, and this morning she made me a wonderful omelette and told me she could never love another man.'

When the Scotsman remains silent, the American smugly asks, 'And how many times did you make love to your wife last night?'

'Once,' he replies. 'Only once?' the Swiss arrogantly snorts. 'And what did she say to you this morning?'

'Don't stop.'

AN ANGRY wife met her husband at the door. There was alcohol on his breath and lipstick on his collar. 'I assume,' she snarled, 'that there is a very good reason for you to come waltzing in here at six o'clock in the morning?' 'There is,' he replied. 'Breakfast.'

A MAN and a woman who have never met before find themselves in the same sleeping carriage of a train. After the initial embarrassment, they both manage to get to sleep, the woman on the top bunk, the man on the lower. In the middle of the night, the woman leans over and says, 'I'm sorry to bother you, but I'm awfully cold and I was wondering if you could possibly pass me another blanket.'

The man leans out and, with a glint in his eye, says, 'I've got a better idea ... let's pretend we're married.'

'Why not,' giggles the woman.

'Good,' he replies. 'Get your own blanket.'

JOHN INVITED his mother for dinner. During the meal, his mother couldn't help but notice how beautiful John's flatmate was. She had long been suspicious of a relationship between John and his flatmate and this only made her more curious. Over the course of the evening, while watching the two interact, she started to wonder if there was more between John and his flatmate than met the eye. Reading his mother's thoughts, John volunteered, 'I know what you must be thinking but I assure you Julie and I are just flatmates.'

About a week later, Julie came to John and said, 'Ever since your mother came to dinner, I've been unable to find the beautiful silver ladle. You don't suppose she took it, do you?' John said, 'Well, I doubt it, but I'll write her a letter just to be sure.' So he sat down and wrote: 'Dear Mother, I am not saying you did take the gravy ladle and I'm not saying you did not take the gravy ladle but the fact remains that one has been missing ever since you were here for dinner. Love John.'

Several days later, John received a letter from his mother which read: 'Dear Son, I'm not saying that you do sleep with Julie and I'm not saying that you do not sleep with Julie but the fact remains that if she was sleeping in her own bed she would have found the gravy ladle by now. Love Mum.'

Lesson of the day: Don't Mess with Mum!

A WOMAN takes a lover during the day while her husband is at work. One day, her nine-year-old son comes home unexpectedly so she puts him in the closet and shuts the door. Then her husband comes home, so she puts her lover in the closet with the little boy.

The little boy says: 'Dark in here.'

The man replies: 'Yes, it is.'

Boy: 'I have a football. Want to buy it?'

Lover: 'No, thanks.'

Boy: 'My dad's outside.'

Lover: 'OK, how much?'

Boy: '£25.'

In the next few weeks, that the boy and his mother's lover find themselves in the closet together again.

Boy: 'Dark in here.'

Lover: 'Yes, it is.'

Boy: 'I have football boots.'

Remembering the last time, the man asks: 'How much?'

Boy: '£75.'

A few days later, the father says to the boy, 'Get on your boots, we'll go and have a game of footy.'

The boy says, 'I can't, I sold them.'

Father: 'How much did you sell them for?'

Boy: '£100.'

The father says, 'That's terrible to overcharge your friends like that. That's way more than those things cost. I'm going to take you to church and make you confess.'

They go to church and the father makes the little boy sit in the confessional and closes the door.

The boy says, 'Dark in here.'

The priest says, 'Don't start that all over again!'

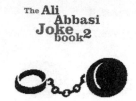

TWO MARRIED blokes are out drinking one night when one turns to the other and says, 'You know, I don't know what else to do. Whenever I go home after we've been out drinking I turn the headlights off before I get to the driveway. I shut off the engine and coast into the garage. I take my shoes off before I go into the house, I sneak up the stairs, I get undressed in the bathroom, I ease into bed and my wife STILL wakes up and says "AND WHAT TIME TO DO YOU CALL THIS?" His mate looks at him and says, 'Well, you're obviously taking the wrong approach. I screech into the driveway, slam the door, storm up the steps, throw my shoes into the closet, jump into bed and say, "How about a quickie?" and she's always sound asleep.'

GUY GOES into a chemists for a packet of condoms and is intrigued by the sight of a special limited edition Sydney 'Olympic' sheaths. He buys a packet and takes them home to his girlfriend. On opening them he discovers that there are three different versions ... bronze, silver and gold.

He says to his girlfriend, 'Shall we try these out? Why don't I wear the gold?'

'How about you wear the silver,' replies his girlfriend, 'I think it's about time someone else came first.'

Marriage is a three-ring circus:
Engagement ring, wedding ring, suffering.

ONE BRIGHT, beautiful Sunday morning, everyone in the tiny town of Johnstown got up early and went to the local church. Before the services started, the townspeople were sitting in their pews and talking about their lives and their families when, suddenly, Satan appeared at the front of the church. Everyone started screaming and running for the front entrance, trampling each other in a frantic effort to get away from evil incarnate.

Soon there was no one left in the church except one elderly gentleman who sat calmly in his pew, not moving ... seemingly ignorant to the fact that God's ultimate enemy was in his presence. Now this confused Satan a bit, so he walked up to the man and said:

'Don't you know who I am?'

The man replied, 'Yes, I do'

Satan asked, 'Aren't you afraid of me?'

'No, I'm not,' said the man.

Satan was a little perturbed and asked, 'Why aren't you afraid of me?'

The man replied, 'I've been married to your sister for over 48 years!'

WALKING INTO the bar, Harry says to the bartender, 'Pour me a stiff one, Eddie, I just had another fight with my wife.'

'Oh yeah?' asks Eddie. 'And how'd this one end?'

'When it was over,' Harry replies, 'she came to me on her hands and knees.'

'Really? Now there's a change! What did she say?'

'She said, "Come out from under that bed, you gutless weasel".'

THERE WAS this guy and he had a girlfriend named Lorraine who was very pretty and he liked her a lot. One day he went to work and found that a new girl had started working there. Her name was Clearly and she was absolutely gorgeous. He became quite besotted with Clearly and after a while it became obvious that she was interested in him too. But this guy was a loyal man and he wouldn't do anything with Clearly while he was still going out with Lorraine. He decided that there was nothing left to do but to break up with Lorraine and get it on with Clearly. He planned several times to tell Lorraine but he couldn't bring himself to do it. Then one day they went for a walk along the riverbank when Lorraine slipped and fell in to the river. The current carried her off and she drowned. The guy stopped for a moment by the river and then ran off smiling and singing ...

'I can see Clearly now Lorraine has gone.'

Lists

Here are some real newspaper headlines, collected by journalists from around the world.

1. Deaf College Opens Doors to Hearing
2. Safety Experts Say School Bus Passengers Should Be Belted
3. Drunk Gets Nine Months in Violin Case
4. Survivor of Siamese Twins Joins Parents
5. Farmer Bill Dies in House
6. Man Minus Ear Waives Hearing
7. Prostitutes Appeal to Pope
8. Panda Mating Fails – Veterinarian Takes Over
9. British Left Waffles on Falkland Islands
10. Squad Helps Dog Bite Victim
11. Enraged Cow Injures Farmer with Axe
12. New Vaccine May Contain Rabies
13. Miners Refuse to Work after Death
14. Juvenile Court to Try Shooting Defendant
15. Stolen Painting Found by Tree
16. Two Sisters Reunited after 18 Years in Checkout Counter
17. Never Withhold Herpes Infection from Loved One
18. Local High School Dropouts Cut in Half
19. If Strike isn't Settled Quickly, It May Last a While
20. Cold Wave Linked to Temperatures
21. Couple Slain – Police Suspect Homicide

22. Red Tape Holds Up New Bridge
23. Man Struck by Lightning Faces Battery Charge
24. New Study of Obesity Looks for Larger Test Group
25. Astronaut Takes Blame for Gas in Spacecraft
26. Kids Make Nutritious Snacks
27. Chef Throws His Heart into Helping Feed Needy
28. Arson Suspect is Held in Massachusetts Fire
29. British Union Finds Dwarfs in Short Supply

And some interesting anagrams ...

Dormitory: 'Dirty room'
Evangelist: 'Evil's agent'
Desperation: 'A rope ends it'
The morse code: 'Here come dots'
Slot machines: 'Cash lost in 'em'
Animosity: 'Is No Amity'
Mother-in-law: 'Woman Hitler'
Snooze alarms: 'Alas! no more Zs'
A decimal point: 'I'm a dot in place'
The earthquakes: 'That queer shake'
Eleven plus two: 'Twelve plus one'

Here are some actual instructions printed on consumer products.

On a blanket from Taiwan:
NOT TO BE USED AS PROTECTION FROM A TORNADO.
On a helmet-mounted mirror used by US cyclists:
REMEMBER, OBJECTS IN THE MIRROR ARE ACTUALLY BEHIND YOU.
On a Taiwanese shampoo:
USE REPEATEDLY FOR SEVERE DAMAGE.
On the bottle-top of a (UK) flavoured milk drink:
AFTER OPENING, KEEP UPRIGHT.
On a New Zealand insect spray:
THIS PRODUCT NOT TESTED ON ANIMALS.
In a US guide to setting up a new computer:
TO AVOID CONDENSATION FORMING, ALLOW THE BOXES TO WARM UP TO ROOM TEMPERATURE BEFORE OPENING.
(Sensible, but the instruction was INSIDE the box.)
On a Japanese product used to relieve painful haemorrhoids:
LIE DOWN ON BED AND INSERT POSCOOL SLOWLY UP TO THE PROJECTED PORTION LIKE A SWORD-GUARD INTO ANAL DUCT. WHILE INSERTING POSCOOL FOR APPROXIMATELY 5 MINUTES, KEEP QUIET.
In some countries, on the bottom of Coca-Cola bottles:
OPEN OTHER END.
On a packet of raisins:
WHY NOT TRY TOSSING OVER YOUR FAVOURITE BREAKFAST CEREAL?
On a hairdryer:
DO NOT USE WHILE SLEEPING.
On a bag of crisps:
YOU COULD BE A WINNER! NO PURCHASE NECESSARY. DETAILS INSIDE.

On a bar of soap:
>DIRECTIONS: USE LIKE REGULAR SOAP.

On a Tiramisu dessert (printed on bottom of the box):
>DO NOT TURN UPSIDE DOWN.

On a bread pudding:
>PRODUCT WILL BE HOT AFTER HEATING.

On a Korean kitchen knife:
>WARNING! KEEP OUT OF CHILDREN.

On a string of Chinese-made Christmas lights:
>FOR INDOOR OR OUTDOOR USE ONLY.

On a Japanese food processor:
>NOT TO BE USED FOR THE OTHER USE.

On a packet of peanuts:
>WARNING – CONTAINS NUTS.

On another packet of nuts:
>INSTRUCTIONS – OPEN PACKET, EAT NUTS.

On a Swedish chainsaw:
>DO NOT ATTEMPT TO STOP CHAIN WITH YOUR
>HANDS OR GENITALS.

On a child's superman costume:
>WEARING OF THIS GARMENT DOES NOT ENABLE YOU TO FLY.

On some frozen dinners:
>SERVING SUGGESTION: DEFROST.

On a hotel provided shower cap in a box:
>FITS ONE HEAD.

On packaging for a iron:
>DO NOT IRON CLOTHES ON BODY.

On Boot's 'Children's' cough medicine:
>DO NOT DRIVE CAR OR OPERATE MACHINERY.

On a sleep aid:
>WARNING! MAY CAUSE DROWSINESS.

Some American bumper stickers.

If you can read this, I can slam on my brakes and sue you!

Jesus loves you, but everyone else thinks you're an asshole.

You're just jealous because the voices are talking to me and not you!

Don't piss me off. I'm running out of places to hide the bodies!

Grow your own dope, plant a man!

Some people are only alive because it is illegal to shoot them.

I used to have a handle on life, but it broke.

Beauty is in the eye of the beer holder.

The more you complain, the longer God makes you live.

IRS: We've got what it takes to take what you've got.

Hard work has a future payoff. Laziness pays off now.

... Back in five minutes. Hang up and drive.

I took an IQ test and the results were negative

Where there's a will ... I want to be named in it.

It's lonely at the top, but you eat better.

And some practical hints and tips:

Give up smoking by sticking one cigarette from each new pack up a friend's bum, filter first, then replacing it in the box. The possibility of putting that one in your mouth will put you off smoking any of them.

Manchester United fans. Save money on expensive new kits by simply strapping a large fake penis to your forehead. It is now clear to all as to your allegiance.

Avoid cutting yourself while clumsily slicing vegetables by getting someone else to hold them while you chop away.

Keep the seat next to you on the train vacant by smiling and nodding at people as they walk up the aisle.

Save on booze by drinking cold tea instead of whisky. The following morning you can create the effects of a hangover by drinking a thimble full of washing-up liquid and banging your head repeatedly on the wall.

Recreate the fun of a visit to a public swimming pool in your own home by filling the bath with cold water, adding two bottles of bleach, then urinating into it, before jumping in.

X-Files fans. Create the effect of being abducted by aliens by drinking two bottles of vodka: you'll invariably wake up in a strange place the following morning, having had your memory mysteriously 'erased'.

Minor skin grafts can be performed on pigs by covering any cuts and grazes with thin strips of bacon.

Don't waste money buying expensive binoculars. Simply stand closer to the object you wish to view.

Avoid jet lag by simply taking an earlier flight, thus arriving fully refreshed and on time.

Save time when crossing a one-way street by only looking in the direction of oncoming traffic.

Thicken up runny low-fat yoghurt by stirring in a spoonful of lard.

A next door neighbour's car aerial, carefully folded, makes an ideal coat hanger in an emergency.

Due to increasing product liability litigation, beer brewers have accepted the Health Executive's suggestion that the following warning labels be placed immediately on all alcohol containers.

WARNING: The consumption of alcohol may make you think you are whispering when you are not.

WARNING: The consumption of alcohol is a major factor in dancing like an idiot.

WARNING: The consumption of alcohol may cause you to think you can sing.

WARNING: The consumption of alcohol may lead you to believe that ex-lovers are really dying for you to telephone them at four in the morning.

WARNING: The consumption of alcohol may make you think you can logically converse with members of the opposite sex without spitting and/or dribbling.

WARNING: The consumption of alcohol may make you think you have mystical Kung Fu powers, resulting in you getting your arse kicked.

WARNING: The consumption of alcohol may cause you to roll over in the morning and see something really scary.

WARNING: The consumption of alcohol is the leading cause of inexplicable tough burns on the forehead.

WARNING: The consumption of alcohol may create the illusion that you are tougher, smarter, faster and better looking than most people.

WARNING: The consumption of alcohol may lead you to believe you are invisible.

WARNING: The consumption of alcohol may lead you to think people are laughing WITH you.

WARNING: The consumption of alcohol may cause a disturbance in the time-space continuum, whereby gaps of time may seem to literally disappear.

WARNING: The consumption of alcohol may cause pregnancy.

One liners

WHAT IS a vampire's favourite sport?
Casketball.

WHAT IS a vampire's favourite holiday?
Fangsgiving.

WHAT DO you get when you cross a vampire and a snowman?
Frostbite.

WHAT IS Dracula's favourite kind of coffee?
Decoffinated.

WHY DO pipers walk when they're playing?
To get away from the noise.

WHAT DID the egg say to the boiling water?
It might take me a while to get hard, I just got laid this morning.

WHAT DO Kodak and condoms have in common?
They both capture the moment.

HOW MANY social workers does it take to change a light bulb?
None, but it takes 15 to write a paper called
'Coping with Darkness'.

TWO AERIALS meet on a roof – fall in love – get married.
The ceremony was rubbish but the reception was brilliant.

A MAN walked into the doctors. The doctor said:
'I haven't seen you in a long time.'
The man replied, 'I know, I've been ill.'

A MAN walks into the doctors and says, 'I've hurt my arm in several places.' The doctor says, 'Well don't go there any more.'

I HAD a ploughman's lunch the other day. He wasn't very happy.

YOU KNOW those mangetout?
They're really nice but I couldn't eat a whole one.

MY DOG was barking at everyone the other day.
Still, what can you expect from a cross-breed?

I WAS driving down the motorway with my girlfriend the other day when we both got a bit frisky and decided to do something about it.
So we decided we'd take the next exit ... but it was a turn-off.

I WENT to buy some camouflage trousers the other day but I couldn't find any.

I BOUGHT some HP sauce the other day.
It's costing me six pence a month for the next two years!

I WENT to the butchers the other day and I bet him 50 quid that he couldn't reach the meat off the top shelf.
He said, 'No, I think the steaks are too high.'

A MAN goes to the doctors with a strawberry growing out of his head.
The Doctor says, 'I'll give you some cream to put on it.'

TWO ELEPHANTS walk off a cliff ... boom boom!

WHAT'S BROWN and sounds like a bell?
DUNG!

TWO HYDROGEN atoms walk into a bar.
     One says, 'I think I've lost an electron.'
The other says 'Are you sure?'
     The first says, 'Yes, I'm positive ... '

TWO FAT blokes are sitting in a pub, one says to the other,
     'Your round.'
     The other one says, 'So are you!'

TWO CANNIBALS are eating a clown.
     One says to the other, 'Does this taste funny to you?'

WHAT DO you call a fish with no eyes?
     A fsh.

HOW DO you get a one-armed Irishman out of a tree?
     Wave to him.

WHAT DO you call a politician who has just lost an election?
A consultant.

WHAT IS the definition of a 'plick'?
Someone who does a runner from a Chinese restaurant.

WHAT DO you call a boomerang that doesn't come back?
A stick.

DIFFERENCE BETWEEN modern politics and a kindergarten?
Adult supervision.

WHAT DO you call a politician driving through a working-class area?
Lost.

WHAT DO light and hard have in common?
You can't sleep with a light on either.

WHERE DO baby apes sleep?
Apricots.

WHAT DO you get if you cross a pig with a zebra?
Stripy sausages.

WHAT DO you call a man in the sea with no arms and no legs?
Bob.

DID YOU hear about the Magic Tractor?
It turned into a field.

WHAT DO you call a man with a spade on his head?
Doug.

WHAT DO you call a man without a spade on his head?
Douglas.

WHAT DO you call a man hiding under a pile of leaves?
    Russell.

HOW DO you know there's elephants in the fridge?
    Footprints in the butter.

WHAT GOES clumpety, clumpety, bonk?
    A centipede with a wooden leg.

A THREE-legged dog walks into a saloon and says:
    'A'm lookin' fer the man what shot ma paw.'

WHAT DO you call a woman with three pints of beer on her head?
    Beatrix.

WHAT DO you call a woman with three pints of beer on her head, playing pool?

Beatrix Potter.

WHAT DO you call a mushroom who buys you drinks?

A fun guy to be with.

WHY DO communists only drink herbal tea?

Because all proper tea is theft.

THERE'S TWO cows in the field – which one's going on holiday?

The one with the wee calf.

WHAT'S YELLOW and stupid?

Thick custard.

WHAT KIND of monkeys make great wine?

Gray apes!

ARE YOU musical?

Well, when I was two I could play on the linoleum!

WHAT DO you call a man who breaks into a meat factory?

A ham burglar.

WHY DID the scarecrow win the Nobel prize?

Because he was outstanding in his field.

ONE-TWO-three cat and un-deux-trois cat are having a race across the Channel – which one wins?

One-two-three cat, because un-deux-trois cat sank.

WHAT'S EIGHT feet tall, green and sits in the corner?

The incredible sulk.

WHY'S THERE no aspirin in the jungle?
Because the parrots eat them all.

WHAT'S RED and invisible?
No tomatoes.

WHAT BEES give us milk?
Boobees.

WHAT DO you have to study to make lemonade?
Fizzyology.

WHAT'S THE fastest drink in the world?
Milk, because it's pasteurised in seconds.

WHAT DO you call an annoying vampire?
A bloody pain in the neck.

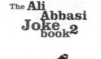

WHAT DO you call a fly that has no wings?
A walk.

WHAT DO you call a sheep that has no legs?
A cloud.

WHY DO you never get hungry at the beach?
Because of the sand which is there.

WHAT'S THE difference between the numbers six and seven?
One.

DID YOU hear about the guy who stayed up all night to find out where the sun went?
It finally dawned on him.

WHAT WOULD people say if you were to jump off one of the bridges and swim in the river that runs though Paris?

That you are insane.

IF ALL the people in the world were laid end-to-end in a circle around the world, they wouldn't like it.

WHY DIDN'T the sesame seed leave the gambling casino?

Because it was on a roll.

THERE WERE three guys walking down the street. Two of them walked into a bar. The third one ducked.

WHAT COLOUR is a hiccup?

Burple!

Did you hear about the boy who had Egyptian flu?
He caught it off his Mummy

DID YOU hear about the pimp who couldn't spell?
He bought a warehouse.

WHAT'S GREEN, lives in a field and has a thousand legs?
Grass, I lied about the legs.

A MAN goes to the doctor and says, 'Doctor, doctor, I've got a lettuce stuck up my bum!'
The doctor replies, 'Well, that's just the tip of the iceberg.'

DID YOU hear about the brave grape?
An elephant stood on it and it only gave a little whine.

HOW CAN you get four suits for a pound?
Buy a deck of cards.

HOW DO dinosaurs pay their bills?
  With Tyrannosaurus cheques.

WHAT DO you call a dinosaur that smashes everything in its path?
  Tyrannosaurus wrecks.

WHAT DO you call a dinosaur that wears a cowboy hat and boots?
  Tyrannosaurus Tex.

DID YOU hear about the red ship and the blue ship that collided?
  Both crews were marooned.

WHY DID Santa's little helper feel depressed?
  He had low elf esteem.

DID YOU hear about the new Divorce Barbie?
  It comes with all of Ken's stuff.

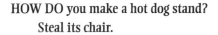

HOW DO you make a hot dog stand?
Steal its chair.

A MAN walks into a doctor's office and says to the receptionist,
'I think I am invisible.'
The receptionist replies, 'I don't think the doctor will be able to
see you.'

TWO FONTS walk into a bar.
The barman says, 'We don't serve your type in here.'

A MAN goes into the bakers and asks, 'Is that a doughnut in the
window or a meringue?'
The baker replies, 'No you're right, it's a doughnut.'

HOW DO you get down from an elephant?
You don't. You get down from a duck.

HOW DO you stay cool at a football match?
Stand next to a fan.

WHAT DO John the Baptist and Kermit the Frog have in common?
The same middle name.

WHAT'S GREY, has four legs and a trunk?
A mouse going on holiday.

WHAT'S BROWN, has four legs and a truck?
A mouse coming back from holiday.

WHAT GOES putt, putt, putt, putt?
A bad golfer.

Animals

DEREK THE prawn is talking to his friend Christian. 'I'm fed up with being a prawn. All we do is eat crud and scuttle under rocks to hide from things. I'd love to be a shark or something, and do something exciting for a change.'

Christian thinks for a while and says, 'Go and talk to the cod. He is very wise, and may be able to help you.'

Derek says, 'Great!' and swims off.

He finds the cod, and tells him of his problem. The cod just wiggles his nose, and Derek the prawn is instantly transformed into a large shark. Derek swims off excitedly, and starts going round eating fish, chasing things, upsetting boats, and generally being a voracious predator.

Eventually (as the cod knew would happen) all the other animals in the sea hide from him, and he gets lonely. He goes back to the cod, and says, 'I've learnt my lesson – please turn me back.'

The cod does, and Derek scuttles off calling: 'Christian – I'm back.'

All he hears is a distant voice shouting, 'I'm not coming near you Derek, you're a vicious killer.'

Derek replies: 'It's all right – I've talked to Cod, and I'm a prawn again, Christian.'

THREE TURTLES, Joe, Steve, and Raymond, decide to go on a picnic. So Joe packs the picnic basket with cookies, bottled sodas, and sandwiches. The trouble is, the picnic site is ten miles away, so the turtles take ten whole days to get there. By the time they do arrive, everyone's exhausted. Joe takes the stuff out of the basket, one by one. He takes out the sodas and says, 'Alright, Steve, gimme the bottle opener.'

'I didn't bring the bottle opener,' Steve says. 'I thought you packed it.' Joe gets worried. He turns to Raymond. 'Raymond, do you have the bottle opener?' Raymond doesn't have it, so the turtles are stuck ten miles away from home without soda. Joe and Steve beg Raymond to turn back home and retrieve it, but Raymond flatly refuses, knowing that they'll eat everything by the time he gets back.

After about two hours, the turtles manage to convince Raymond to go, swearing on their great-grand turtles' graves that they won't touch the food. So, Raymond sets off down the road, slow and steadily. Twenty days pass, but no Raymond. Joe and Steve are hungry and puzzled, but a promise is a promise. Another day passes, and still no Raymond, but a promise is promise. After three more days pass without Raymond in sight, Steve starts getting restless. 'I NEED FOOD!' he says with a hint of dementia in his voice. 'NO!' Joe retorts. 'We promised.' Five more days pass. Joe realises that Raymond probably skipped out to the diner down the road, so the two turtles weakly lift the lid, get out sandwiches, and open their mouths to eat.

But then, right at that instant, Raymond pops out from behind a rock, and says, 'I knew it! I'm not going.'

A SUNDAY league football team is so desperate for players that one Sunday they are forced to play with a chicken in their team. Surprisingly, the chicken has a brilliant first half. One minute it's clearing off its own line, the next putting in a perfect cross.

At half time all the team mates are very pleased and everyone runs back onto the pitch for the second half. On the way the ref starts chatting to the chicken. 'Great first half mate.'

'Thanks,' replies the chicken, 'I try to keep myself fit. It's difficult finding time, but I do an hour in the gym each morning before work.' 'What do you do?' asks the ref.

'I'm a chartered accountant,' comes the reply. At which point the referee brandishes the red card and sends the chicken off. The bemused team mates gather round and start complaining to the referee.

'Sorry lads,' says the referee, 'I had no choice. Professional fowl.'

A TURKEY is standing in a field chatting to a bull. 'I would love to be able to get to the top of yonder tree,' sighs the turkey, 'but I haven't got the energy.'

'Well, why don't you nibble on some of my droppings?' replies the bull. 'They're packed with nutrients.'

The turkey pecks at a lump of dung and finds that it actually gives him enough strength to reach the first branch of the tree. The next day, after eating some more dung, he reaches the second branch. And so on. Finally after a fortnight, there he is, proudly perched at the top of the tree. Whereupon he's spotted by a farmer who dashes into the farmhouse, emerges with a shotgun, and shoots the turkey right out of the tree.

Moral of the story: bullshit might get you to the top, but it won't keep you there.

DECLAN THE humble crab and Kate the lobster princess were madly, deeply and passionately in love. For months they enjoyed an idyllic relationship, until one day Kate scuttled over to Declan in tears. 'We can't see each other anymore ... ' she sobbed. 'Why?' gasped Declan. 'Daddy says that crabs are too common,' she wailed. 'He claims you, a mere crab, and a poor one at that, are the lowest class of crustacean. No daughter of his will marry someone who can only walk sideways.'

Declan was shattered, and scuttled away into the darkness to drink himself into a filthy state of aquatic oblivion. That night the great lobster ball was taking place. Lobsters came from far and wide dancing and merry making, but the lobster princess refused to join in, choosing instead to sit by her father's side, inconsolable.

Suddenly, the doors burst open, and Declan the crab strode in. The lobsters all stopped their dancing, the princess gasped and the king lobster rose from his throne. Slowly, painstakingly, Declan the crab made his way across the floor. All could see that he was walking FORWARDS, one claw after another! Step by step he made his approach towards the throne, until he finally looked king lobster in the eye. There was a deadly hush.

Finally, the crab spoke ... 'God, I'm drunk.'

A MAN walks into a restaurant and orders squid. 'Certainly Sir,' says Jervaise the waiter, 'would you like to choose your squid from the tank over there?'

'I'll have that little green one with the moustache,' says the customer.

'Oh no!' replies Jervaise, 'but he's my favourite! He's so small and cute and friendly. Surely you'd prefer one of the bigger, meatier ones?'

'No,' says the customer. 'It's got to be that one.'

So Jervaise gets the little green squid out and puts him on the chopping block and raises his knife. The little squid looks up and smiles, twitching his bushy moustache into a big friendly grin!

'It's no good,' says Jervaise, 'I can't do it. I'll have to ask Hans, the guy who does the washing up. He's a big, tough brute – he'll be able to do the evil deed.' So out comes Hans, while Jervaise disappears off in tears. Hans picks up the knife, raises it to chop the little squid's head off and once again the little friendly squid looks up and smiles, wiggling his little legs and twitching his little moustache. Hans finds it impossible to kill him too.

So ... Hans that does dishes is as soft as Jervaise with mild green hairy-lipped squid.

A POLAR bear walks into bar and says to barman 'Can I have a gin ... ... and tonic please'.

Barman says, 'Sure but why the big pause?'

'Oh!' says the bear, 'they're great for catching salmon!'

THERE'S THIS man, John, who really, really wants a pet. He's not allowed to keep dogs, cats or rodents in his rented house, and isn't really keen on fish, so he's a little bit stuck.

One day John decides to just go to the pet shop to see if they can help. He explains his predicament to the owner who says, 'D'you know, I have the perfect pet for you, wait here and I'll go and get him.' He comes back a couple of minutes later with a centipede in his hand.

Poor John just can't hide the disappointment from his face. 'A centipede wasn't really what I had in mind,' he apologises.

'Aaah, but this isn't any old centipede,' the shop owner tells him, 'this is a very special centipede – he'll do anything for you. He'll cook and clean and tell you very good jokes. Tell you what, why don't you take him home for a week, and if the two of you truly are incompatible, you are welcome to bring him back.'

As he has absolutely nothing to lose, and because he so wants a pet, John takes the centipede home (a bargain at three pounds) and names him Jim. John's quite tired after all the day's excitement, so he goes for a quick snooze. When he wakes up an hour later, Jim has dusted and polished the whole house, cleaned the windows, done all the washing and there's a cup of steaming hot tea waiting by his side. John is so pleased – he can't believe how fantastic Jim is! He goes to thank Jim, and finds him going through the cupboards.

'What are you doing, Jim?' he asks.

'Just wondering what to make for tea,' comes the reply.

'Look, as it's our first night together, why don't we have fish and chips.' Jim offers to go for them, and John gives him the money and off he pops.

An hour passes, and John's starting to get really hungry. Two hours pass and he starts to get worried. He puts on his jacket and opens the door. Only to find Jim still on the doorstep.

'What are you doing, Jim? You went outside over two hours ago!'

Jim looks up and sighs, 'I'm just putting on my shoes!'

A BEAR walks into a bar and sits down. He bangs on the bar with his paw and demands a beer.

The barman approaches and says, 'We don't serve beer to bears in bars in Billings, Montana.'

The bear, becoming angry, once again demands a beer.

The barman again tells him, 'We don't serve beer to bears in bars in Billings, Montana.'

The bear, very angry now, says, 'If you don't serve me a beer, I'm going to eat that lady sitting at the end of the bar.'

The barman once again says, 'Sorry, we don't serve beer to bears in bars in Billings, Montana.'

The bear goes to the end of the bar and, as he has threatened, eats the woman. He comes back to his seat, and again demands a beer.

The barman says, 'Sorry, we don't serve beer to bears in bars in Billings, Montana, that are on drugs.'

The bear says, 'I'm not on drugs.'

The barman says, 'Yes you are. That was a bar bitch you ate.'

A DUCK walks into a bar and asks the barman, 'Do you have any food? The barman replies, 'No, we don't serve food here.' So the duck leaves.

The next day the duck walks into the bar again and asks the barman, 'You got any food.' The barman says, 'No, we don't serve food here.' So the duck leaves.

The next day the duck walks into the bar again and asks the barman, 'You got any food?' The barman says, 'NO, we don't serve food ... and if you come in here again asking for food I am going to nail you to the wall.' So the duck leaves.

The next day the duck walks into the bar and asks the barman, 'You got any nails?' The barman says, 'No!'

The duck asks, 'You got any food?'

A COUPLE have a pet parrot that they are extremely fond of. One day, when the man is sitting watching the telly, he notices that the parrot has just dropped off its perch. He takes it to his vet who shakes her head on seeing it and proclaims it dead.

The man is distraught, the parrot is only six years old and has always been in great health, so he demands a second opinion. The vet argues with him, but eventually, realising that the man is just really upset, she concedes. Ten minutes later a labrador comes in, sniffs the parrot and shakes his head.

'I'm afraid that's your second opinion. The parrot is definitely dead.' says the vet.

The man is outraged, 'This is ridiculous. How can I rely on the opinion of a labrador?' he screams. 'I need a third opinion. And I don't want another dog!'

Again the vet argues, but once again, eventually concedes. Five minutes later a cat comes in, picks up the parrot, sniffs it and shakes its head. The vet follows the cat out of the room, promising to be back soon.

She returns a couple of minutes later. 'Well we've now got the results of the lab report and the cat scan ...'

ALISON GETS a new job as an assistant at the zoo. Her main duty is to clean out the animals' cages at the end of the day.

On the first day, she is in charge of cleaning out the tropical fish tanks. She realises, too late, that she has put the wrong detergent in the tanks, and that she's killed the fish. She is very upset and doesn't know what to do. If she owns up, she'll surely lose her job. She then has a brainwave – she will conceal the evidence by feeding the dead fish to the lions. So she does.

The next day, she is feeding the chimps. The chimps are none too happy as they had been fed stale cakes for their tea party. They decide to take their anger out on Alison, who retaliates. Unfortunately, she goes a bit too far and kills two of the chimps. Now, Alison is worried, but not as much as she had been the day before, as she's discovered a great way of concealing the evidence. So, she goes to the lions' cage and feeds them the dead chimps.

The next day, Alison is cleaning out the bees when they begin to swarm. Terrified, Alison sprays the angry swarm with a very strong deodorant she has in her bag, then squashes them with a stick, killing every last bee. Again, she runs off to the lions' cage and feeds the dead bees to the lions.

A couple of days after the bee incident, a new lion comes to the zoo. As soon as the zoo keeper lets him into the cage with the other lions, he starts chatting, 'So lads, what's this zoo like, then? Do they treat you well?' 'Well,' says the head of the zoo's pride. 'It's just fantastic here. We get so well fed. You know, in the last week we've had fish and chimps and mushy bees!'

THERE WAS an old magician who worked on a cruise ship on the Pacific. He'd been a very famous and highly revered magician in his time, but his show was getting very, very tired. What made it even worse, though, was that he had a pet parrot who'd seen all his tricks a million times before and had figured them out. At every show, the parrot would tell the audience the 'magic' behind the trick:

'It's under the table!'

'There's two women!'

'Trick cards!'

One night, in the middle of the performance, the ship hit an iceberg and sank. Everybody drowned apart from the magician and his parrot. They managed to swim to a piece of wreckage and climb aboard, where the magician collapsed from exhaustion.

The parrot just stared and stared and stared at the magician, who lay unconscious for three days. Eventually, the magician stirred. Looking up, he saw the parrot, still staring.

Another hour went by and finally the parrot squawked: 'Alright, I give up. What did you do with the ship?'

Idiots and Twits

FINDING ONE of her students making faces at others on the playground, Ms Smith stops to gently reprove the child. Smiling sweetly the teacher says, 'When I was a child, I was told if I made ugly faces I would stay like that.'

The student looks up and replies, 'Well you can't say you weren't warned.'

ANGUS REALLY fancies this girl called Marie. One day he gets up the courage to ask her out on a date. 'I'd be delighted,' she answers.

Angus is so excited he goes round to see his big brother, Hamish, and tells him the news.

'Fantastic,' says Hamish getting out his wallet. 'Here's two pounds to get a chocolate mouse.'

Angus is a bit puzzled: 'Don't you mean chocolate mousse?'

'But I've only given you enough for one dessert!'

AN ENGINEERING student is walking on campus one day when another engineer rides up on a shiny new motorcycle.

'Where did you get such a great bike?' asked the first.

The second engineer replies: 'Well, I was walking along yesterday minding my own business when a beautiful woman rode up on this bike. She threw the bike to the ground, took off all her clothes and said, "Take what you want".'

The second engineer nods approvingly, 'Good choice, the clothes probably wouldn't have fitted.'

AFTER HAVING their eleventh child, a Welsh couple decide that enough is enough. So, the husband goes to his doctor and tells him that he and his wife don't want to have any more children.

The doctor tells him that there is a procedure called a vasectomy that can fix the problem. The doctor instructs him to go home, get a cherry bomb, light it, put it in a beer can, then hold the can up to his ear and count to ten.

The Welshman says to the doctor, 'I may not be the smartest man, but I don't see how putting a cherry bomb in a beer can next to my ear is going to help me.'

So, the couple drive to England to get a second opinion. The English physician is just about to tell them about the procedure for a vasectomy when he notices that they are from Wales. This doctor instead tells the man to go home and get a cherry bomb, light it, place it in a beer can, hold it to his ear and count to ten.

Figuring that both learned physicians couldn't be wrong, the man goes home, lights a cherry bomb and puts it in a beer can. He holds the can up to his ear and begins to count. 'One, two, three, four, five ... ' at which point he pauses, places the beer can between his legs and resumes counting on his other hand ...

AN ENGINEER is crossing a road one day when a frog calls out to him and says, 'If you kiss me, I'll turn into a beautiful princess.' He bends over, picks up the frog and puts it in his pocket. The frog speaks again and says, 'If you kiss me and turn me back into a beautiful princess, I will stay with you for one week.' The engineer takes the frog out of his pocket, smiles at it and returns it to the pocket. The frog then cries out, 'If you kiss me and turn me back into a princess, I'll stay with you and do ANYTHING you want.' Again the engineer takes the frog out, smiles at it and puts it back into his pocket.

Finally, the frog asks, 'What's the matter? I've told you I'm a beautiful princess, that I'll stay with you for a week and do anything you want. Why won't you kiss me?'

The engineer says, 'Look, I'm an engineer, I don't have time for a girlfriend, but a talking frog ... boy, that's cool.'

THERE ARE four engineers travelling in a car – a mechanical engineer, a chemical engineer, an electrical engineer, and a computer engineer. The car breaks down.

'Sounds to me as if the pistons have seized.' says the mechanical engineer. 'We'll have to strip down the engine before we can get the car working again.'

'Well,' says the chemical engineer, 'it sounded to me as if the fuel might be contaminated. I think we should clear out the fuel system.'

'I thought it might be an grounding problem,' says the electrical engineer, 'or maybe a faulty plug lead.'

They all turn to the computer engineer, who up to then has said nothing, and ask him what he thinks.

'Ummm ... perhaps if we all get out of the car and get back in again?'

How many Essex girls does it take to make a chocolate chip cookie?
Five. One to stir the mixture and four to peel the smarties.

What do you call an Essex girl with an IQ of 150?
Basildon.

TWO BLONDES are walking down the street. One notices a make-up compact on the sidewalk and leans down to pick it up. She opens it, looks in the mirror and says, 'Hmm, this person looks familiar.'

The second blonde says, 'Here, let me see!' So the first blonde hands her the compact. The second one looks in the mirror and says, 'You dummy, it's me!'

AFTER TRAVELLING for a few streets, a busty blonde realises she has no money and immediately informs the taxi driver.

'You'd better stop. I can't pay you and it's a fiver already.'

The driver checks her out in the rearview mirror. 'That's okay,' he says. 'I'll turn down the first dark street, get in the back seat and take off your bra.'

'You'd be cheating yourself,' she replies. 'It only cost me two fifty in Asda.'

A BLONDE is bragging about her knowledge of capitals. She proudly says, 'Go ahead, ask me, I know all of them.' A friend says, 'OK, what's the capital of France?' The blonde replies, 'Oh, that's easy: F.'

WHAT DID the blonde say to her doctor when he told her she was pregnant?

'Is it mine?'

A BLONDE and her brunette friend are talking. 'I hate all the blonde jokes people say.'

'Oh, they are only jokes. There are a lot of stupid people out there. Here I'll prove it to you.' So they go outside and hail a taxi. 'Please take me to 29 Nickle Street to see if I'm home,' says the brunette.

The taxi drives them and when they finally get out the brunette looks at the blonde and says. 'See that guy was really stupid.'

'No kidding,' replies the blonde. 'There was a pay-phone just around the corner, you could have called instead!'

A BLONDE and a lawyer are seated next to each other on a flight from London to New York. The lawyer asks if she would like to play a fun game. The blonde, tired, just wants to take a nap, politely declines and rolls over to the window to catch a few winks.

The lawyer persists and explains that the game is easy and a lot of fun. He says, 'I ask you a question, and if you don't know the answer, you pay me five pounds, and vice versa.'

Again, she declines and tries to get some sleep. The lawyer, now agitated, says, 'Okay, if you don't know the answer you pay me five pounds, and if I don't know the answer, I will pay you five hundred pounds.'

This catches the blonde's attention and, figuring there will be no end to this torment unless she plays, she agrees to the game. The lawyer asks the first question. 'What's the distance from the earth to the moon?'

The blonde doesn't say a word, reaches into her purse, pulls out a five pound note and hands it to the lawyer. 'Okay,' says the lawyer, 'your turn.' She asks the lawyer, 'What goes up a hill with three legs and comes down with four legs?'

The lawyer, puzzled, takes out his laptop computer and searches all his references, no answer. He taps into the air phone with his modem and searches the net. No answer.

Frustrated, he sends e-mails to all his friends and colleagues, but to no avail. After an hour, he wakes the blonde, and hands her five hundred pounds. The blonde says, 'Thank you,' and turns back to get some more sleep.

The lawyer, who is more than a little miffed, then asks her, 'Well, what's the answer?' Without a word, the blonde hands him five pounds, and goes back to sleep.

THIS BLONDE was sick and tired of jokes about how dumb blondes are. So she decides to show her husband that she's really smart. While he is at the office, she gets to work and paints a couple of rooms in the house. Her husband arrives home and smells the distinctive aroma of fresh paint. He walks into the living room and finds his wife lying on the floor in a pool of sweat. She is wearing a ski jacket and a fur coat at the same time. When he asks her if she is okay, she replies yes. He asks what she is doing. She replies that she wanted to prove to him that not all blondes are dumb by painting a couple of rooms. He then asks her why she has a ski jacket over her fur coat. She replies that she was reading the directions on the paint tin ... the instructions said ... for best results ... put on two coats.

Sport

THE ALL Blacks were playing England and after the half-time whistle blew they found themselves up by 50 points to nil with Jonah Lomu scoring six tries. The rest of the team decided to go down to the pub instead of playing the second half and told Jonah that he was on his own.

'No problem,' Jonah told the captain, 'I'll come down after the game and report back.'

Well, after the game Jonah found the rest of the team at the pub. 'What was the final score Jonah?' asked one of the players. 'Ninety-five to three,' Jonah replies.

'What!' Exclaimed the captain '... how did you let them get three points????'

Jonah replied ... 'I got sent off with 20 minutes to go.'

THREE POTATO princesses are talking to each other about who they're going to marry.

The first one says, 'I'm going out with King Edward. He'll marry me.'

The second one says, 'I'm seeing a tuber called Spud. He's a bit dirty but where there's muck, there's brass and he's loaded.'

The third one looks a bit upset at this. 'Who are you going out with?' the other potatoes ask.

'Des Lynam,' says the third. 'He's a common-tater.'

DAVID BECKHAM was trying to do a jigsaw puzzle on Friday evening and was getting nowhere so he phoned Sir Alex and the conversation went ...

Beckham: 'Boss, boss I'm trying to complete this jigsaw puzzle and Posh is away, and I don't fink I'll be able to concentrate on the game tomorrow until I finish it.'

Sir Alex: 'Use the picture on the box to help you David.'

Beckham: 'I've tried that but I still can't get the bits to fit together to complete the picture.'

Sir Alex: 'What's the picture of?'

Beckham: 'It's a nice tiger boss. Can I come over and you can help me?'

Sir Alex: 'Aye, alright David.'

Beckham puts all the pieces back in the box and gets into his Ferrari and drives round to Sir Alex's house. They both go into the kitchen with Beckham clutching his jigsaw puzzle.

Sir Alex: 'OK, David put all the pieces on the table, we'll turn them up the right way so we can see them and put the box here so we can copy the picture.'

Beckham empties the pieces out onto the table and props the box up.

Sir Alex looks at the pieces, looks at the box and then looks at Beckham and says, 'David, put the Frosties back in the box.'

DID YOU hear that the Post Office has had to recall their latest stamps. They had pictures of English Rugby players on them. People couldn't figure out which side to spit on.

WHAT DO English Rugby fans and sperm have in common?
One in three million has a chance of becoming a human being.

WHAT DO you have when 100 English Rugby fans are buried up to their necks in sand?
Not enough sand.

General

AN OUT of work ventriloquist goes to his long suffering agent and asks him why all of his gigs have dried up.

'There is no call for vent acts these days,' says the agent. 'You have to change your act. How about becoming a medium? There is a lot of call for that.'

The bloke duly gets a job in a fairground and his first customer turns up asking if its possible to contact her dearly departed. 'Okay madam we have three rates. For twenty quid I contact your late husband and relay his message to you in my voice.'

The woman isn't too keen and enquires after the next rate. 'For forty quid I contact your husband and relay his message to you in his voice'.

The woman, still unimpressed, asks what the third option is and the bloke says, 'For sixty quid, I contact your husband, relay his message to you in his voice whilst drinking a bottle of beer!'

A PROCTOLOGIST walks into a bank. Preparing to endorse a cheque, he pulls a rectal thermometer out of his shirt pocket and tries to write with it.

Realising his mistake, he looks at the thermometer with annoyance and says, 'Well that's great, just great! Some bugger's got my pen!'

ONCE UPON a time, in a land far away, a beautiful, independent, self-assured princess happened upon a frog as she sat contemplating ecological issues on the shores of an unpolluted pond in a verdant meadow near her castle. The frog hopped into the princess' lap and said: 'Elegant Lady, I was once a handsome prince, until an evil witch cast a spell upon me. One kiss from you, however, and I will turn back into the dapper, young prince that I am and then, my sweet, we can marry and set up home in your castle with my mother, where you can prepare my meals, clean my clothes, bear my children, and forever feel grateful and happy doing so.' That night, as the princess dined sumptuously on a repast of lightly sautéed frog legs seasoned in a white wine and onion cream sauce, she chuckled and thought to herself: 'I don't bloody think so!'

A BUSINESSMAN boards a flight and is lucky enough to be seated next to an absolutely gorgeous woman. They exchange brief hellos and he notices she is reading a manual about sexual statistics.

He asks her about it and she replies, 'This is a very interesting book about sexual statistics. It says that American Indians have the longest average penis and Polish men have the biggest average diameter. By the way, my name is Jill. What's yours?'

He coolly replies, 'Tonto Kawalski, nice to meet you.'

A MAN walks into a bar, sits down, and orders a beer. As he sips the beer, he hears a soothing voice say, 'Nice tie.' Looking around, he notices that the bar is empty, except for himself and the barman. A few sips later, the voice says, 'Beautiful shirt.' At this, the man calls the barman over.

'Hey, I must be losing my mind,' he tells the barman. 'I keep hearing these voices saying nice things, and there's not a soul in here but us.'

'It's the peanuts,' answers the barman.

'What?' replies the man in disbelief.

'You heard me,' says the barman. 'It's the peanuts ... they're complimentary.'

So after the peanuts had complimented the guy he wanders off to the toilet. As he is halfway, he hears another voice. Somewhat different from the peanuts, more aggressive.

The voice says 'Where did you get that shirt? ... it's awful!'

The guy (naturally) feels a little put out. Then again he hears ... 'Christ you're ugly aren't you? ... How much grease do you slap on your head each morning?'

Now the guy is getting a little annoyed and starts to look around. Then the voice says, 'You expect to meet a girl looking like that? ... Try a visit to a decent tailors ... and perhaps see if a doctor can rid you of that smell.'

That's it, the guy goes up to the bar and says to the barman, 'OK so who's the wise guy now? There's only you, me and the complimentary peanuts ... but someone is giving me all this abuse!' The barman replies 'Ahhh, that'll be the cigarette machine ... it's out of order!'

MAN is walking home alone late one night when he hears a ......
BUMP ...

BUMP ...

BUMP ... behind him ...

Walking faster he looks back, and makes out the image of an upright coffin banging its way down the middle of the street towards him ...

BUMP ...

BUMP ...

BUMP ...

Terrified, the man begins to run towards his home, the coffin bouncing quickly behind him ...

faster ...

faster ...
...
... BUMP ...
...
.... BUMP ...
...
...
... BUMP.

He runs up to his door, fumbles with his keys, opens the door, rushes in, slams and locks the door behind him.

But ...
the coffin crashes through his door, with the lid of the coffin clapping clappity ... BUMP ...

....

...

... clappity ... BUMP ...

...

... clappity ... BUMP ...

...

... clappity ... BUMP ....

...

on the heels of the terrified man .....

...

Rushing upstairs to the bathroom, the man locks himself in.
His heart is pounding; his head is reeling; his breath is coming in sobbing gasps ...

...

...

With a loud CRASH the coffin breaks down the door.
Bumping and
clapping towards him ....

...

...

The man screams and reaches for something, anything ... but all he can find is a bottle of cough syrup!

...

...

...

Desperate, he throws the cough syrup at the coffin ...

....

...

...

...

... ... the coffin stops.

Two brooms were hanging in the closet and after a while they got to know each other so well, they decided to get married. The bride broom looked very beautiful in her white dress. The groom broom was handsome and suave in his tuxedo. The wedding was lovely. After the wedding, the bride broom leaned over and said to the groom broom, 'I think I am going to have a little whisk broom!'

'IMPOSSIBLE!' said the groom broom, 'we haven't even swept together!'

A FROG walks into the bank, goes up to Patty Whack, the cashier and asks for a loan of £30,000.

Patty looks at the frog in disbelief and asks his name. The frog says his name is Kermit Jagger, his dad is Mick Jagger, and that it's okay, he knows the bank manager. Patty explains that he will need to secure the loan with some collateral.

The frog says, 'Sure. I have this,' and produces a tiny porcelain elephant, about half an inch tall – bright pink and perfectly formed.

Very confused, Patty explains that she'll have to consult with the bank manager and disappears into a back office.

She finds the manager and says, 'There's a frog called Kermit Jagger out there who claims to know you and wants to borrow £30,000 and he wants to use this as collateral.'

She holds up the tiny pink elephant. 'I mean, what in the world is this?'

The bank manager looks back at her and says ...

'It's a knick-knack, Patty Whack. Give the frog a loan. His old man's a Rolling Stone.'

THERE ONCE was a successful rancher who died and left everything to his wife. She was determined to keep the ranch and make a go of it, but she knew very little about ranching, so she decided to place an ad in the newspaper for a ranch hand. Two men applied for the job. One was gay and the other a drunk. She decided to hire the gay guy, figuring it would be safer to have him around the house than the drunk. He turned out to be fantastic worker. He worked long, hard hours every day and knew a lot about ranching. For eight weeks the two of them worked, and the ranch was doing really well.

Then one day the rancher's wife said to the hired hand, 'You've done a really good job and the ranch looks great, you should go into town and kick up your heels.'

The hired hand agreed readily, and on Saturday night went in to town. However, one o'clock came and he didn't return. Two o'clock, and still no hired hand.

At two thirty, he finally came home. The rancher's wife was sitting by the fireplace and quietly called him over to her. 'Unbutton my blouse and take it off,' she said. Trembling, he did as she asked.

'Now take off my boots.' He did so, slowly.

'Now take off my socks.' He did.

'Now take off my skirt.' He did.

'Now take off my bra.' Again with trembling hands he did as she asked.

'Now,' she said, 'take off my panties.' He slowly pulled them down. Then she looked at him and said, 'Don't you ever wear my clothes to town again!'

YOU KNOW, somebody actually complimented me on my driving today. They left a little note on the windscreen. It said 'Parking Fine'. So that was nice.

ONE DAY in the Garden of Eden, Eve calls out to God. 'Lord, I have a problem!'

'What's the problem, Eve?'

'Lord, I know you created me and provided this beautiful garden and all of these wonderful animals and that hilarious comedy snake, but I'm just not happy.'

'Why is that, Eve?' came the reply from above.

'Lord, I am lonely, and I'm sick to death of apples.'

'Well, Eve, in that case, I have a solution. I shall create a man for you.'

'What's a man, Lord?'

'Man is to be a flawed creature, with many bad traits. He'll lie, cheat, and be vain; all in all, he'll give you a hard time. But he'll be bigger, faster, and will like to hunt and kill things. He will look silly when he's aroused, but since you've been complaining, I'll create him in such a way that he will satisfy your physical needs. He will be witless and will revel in childish things like fighting and kicking a ball about. He won't be too smart, so he'll also need your advice to think properly.'

'Sounds great,' says Eve, with an ironically raised eyebrow. 'What's the catch, Lord?'

'Well ... you can have him on one condition.'

'What's that, Lord?'

'As I said, he'll be proud, arrogant, and self-admiring ... so you'll have to let him believe that I made him first. Just remember, it's our little secret ... you know, woman to woman.'

AFTER QUASIMODO'S death, the bishop of the cathedral of Notre Dame sends word through the streets of Paris that a new bell ringer is needed. After observing several applicants demonstrate their skills, the bishop decides to call it a day. Just then, an armless man approaches him and announces that he has come to apply for the job.

The bishop is incredulous. 'You have no arms!' 'No matter,' says the man. 'Observe!' And begins striking the bells with his face, producing a beautiful melody on the carillon. The bishop listens in astonishment; convinced he's finally found a replacement for Quasimodo. But suddenly, rushing forward to strike a bell, the armless man trips and plunges headlong to his death in the street below. The stunned bishop rushes to his side. When he reaches the street, a crowd has gathered around the fallen figure, drawn by the beautiful music they had heard only moments before.

As they silently part to let the bishop through, one of them asks, 'Bishop, who was this man?' 'I don't know his name,' the bishop sadly replies, 'but his face rings a bell.'

The following day, despite the sadness that weighs heavily on his heart due to the unfortunate death of the armless campanologist, the bishop continues his interviews for the bell ringer of Notre Dame.

The first man to approach him says, 'Your Excellency, I am the brother of the poor armless wretch that fell to his death from this very belfry yesterday. I pray that you honour his life by allowing me to replace him in this duty.'

The bishop agrees to give the man an audition, and, as the armless man's brother stoops to pick up a mallet to strike the first bell, he groans, clutches at his chest, twirls around, and dies on the spot.

Two monks, hearing the bishop's cries of grief at this second tragedy, rushed up the stairs to his side. 'What has happened? Who is this man?' the first monk asked breathlessly.

'I don't know his name,' sighed the distraught bishop, but ... he's a dead ringer for his brother.'

A HUGE muscular man walks into a bar and orders a beer. The barman hands him the beer and says, 'You know, I'm not gay or anything but I want to compliment you on your physique, it really is phenomenal! I have a question though, why is your head so small?'

The big guy nods slowly. He's obviously been asked this question many times. 'One day,' he begins, 'I was hunting when I got lost in the woods. I heard someone crying for help and finally realised that it was coming from a frog sitting next to a stream. So I picked up the frog, and it said, "Kiss me. Kiss me and I will turn into a genie and grant you three wishes." So I looked around to make sure I was alone and gave the frog a kiss. POOF! The frog turned into a beautiful, voluptuous, naked woman. She said, "You now have three wishes." I looked down at my scrawny 115 pound body and said, "I want a body like Arnold Schwarzenegger." She nodded, whispered a spell, and POOF! there I was, so huge that I ripped out of my clothes and was standing there naked!

'She then asked, "What will be your second wish?" I looked hungrily at her beautiful body and replied, "I want to make sensuous love with you here by this stream." She nodded, lay down, and beckoned to me. We then made love for hours!

'As we lay there next to each other, sweating from our glorious lovemaking, she whispered into my ear, "You know, you do have one more wish. What will it be?"

'I looked at her and replied, "How about a little head?" '

TWO PRIESTS go to Hawaii on holiday and decide that they'll make this a real holiday by not wearing anything that would identify them as clergy. As soon as the plane lands, they head for a store and buy some really outrageous shorts, shirts, sandals, and sunglasses.

The next morning, they're on the beach, dressed in their 'tourist' garb and sitting on beach chairs, enjoying a drink, the sunshine and the scenery when a drop dead gorgeous blonde in a tiny bikini comes walking straight towards them. They can't help but stare and when she passes them she turns, smiles and says, 'Good morning father, good morning father,' nodding and addressing each of them individually, then passes on by. They're both stunned – how in the world did she recognise them as priests?

The next day they went again to the store, buy even more outrageous outfits – so loud, you could hear them before you could even see them – and again they settle on the beach in their chairs to enjoy the sunshine.

After a while, the same gorgeous blonde, wearing a string bikini this time, comes toward them. (They were glad they had sunglasses, because their eyes were about to pop out of their heads.) She approaches them and greets them individually: 'Good morning father ... good morning father,' and starts to walk away.

One of the priests can't stand it and says, 'just a minute young lady. Yes we are priests, and proud of it, but I have to know, how in the world do YOU know?'

'Oh father, don't you recognise me – I'm Sister Kathryn!'

A MAN in a bar has a couple of beers, and the barman tells him he owes three pounds. 'But I paid, don't you remember?' says the customer. 'Okay,' says the barman. 'If you say you paid, you did.' The man then goes outside and tells a friend that the barman can't keep track of his customers' bills.

The second man then rushes in and orders a beer. When it's time to pay he pulls the same stunt. The barman replies, 'If you say you paid, I'll take your word for it.'

Soon the customer goes into the street, sees an old friend, and tells him how to get free drinks. The man hurries into the bar and begins to drink high balls when, suddenly, the barman leans over and says, 'You know, a funny thing happened in here tonight. Two men were drinking beer, neither paid and both claimed that they did. The next guy who tries that is going to get punched right in the nose.'

'Don't bother me with your troubles,' the final patron responds. 'Just give me my change and I'll be on my way.'

THE ORIGAMI Bank has folded, the Sumo Bank has gone belly up and the Bonsai Bank plans to cut back some of its branches. Insider reports say that the Karaoke Bank is up for sale, and is going for a song. Meanwhile, shares in the Kamikaze Bank have nose-dived and 500 back-office staff at the Karate Bank got the chop. Analysts report that there is something fishy going on at the Sushi Bank and staff there fear that they may get a raw deal.

DARTH VADER has finally trapped Luke Skywalker, and they are about commence their battle in Cloud City. The air is electric with tension, there is a deathly silence all around them save for Vader's breathing, and the buzzing of the lightsabres, when Vader says to Luke:

'Luke ... I know something you don't know.'

'What do you know Vader.'

'I know a secret that you are dying to find out ...'

'Tell me, Vader.'

'Luke ... I know what you are getting for Christmas.'

'Impossible! How do you know this?'

'I felt your presents ...'

A MAN walks into the doctors and says, 'Doctor, doctor, you have to help me. On Wednesdays and Thursdays I think I'm a teepee and on Fridays and Saturdays I think I'm a Wigwam.

The doctor replies, 'Don't worry, I think you're just too tense!'

Readers' Jokes

These jokes were submitted by readers of the *Sunday Post*.

Peter Dennis from Clynder sent in the following thirteen!

TWO LADIES on holiday in Cannes are chatting in a café, when one says to the other, 'That must be the biggest diamond ring in the world you are wearing.' 'Indeed it is,' says the second lady, 'This is Jones' diamond, from South Africa, and it is supposed to be the largest diamond in the world. Unfortunately, with the Jones' diamond comes the Jones' curse.' 'Oh dear,' says the first lady, 'please tell me what is the Jones' curse.' The second lady looks at her diamond and sighs, 'Mr Jones.'

'NOAH,' SAID God, 'there will be enormous floods next year, and this time I want no animals on your Arc, just fish. And not any old fish, but carp in glass tanks. This time I want you to build an Ark that's very big, say at least seven or eight decks high'. 'I've got you Lord,' says Noah, 'What you want is a multi-storey carp ark.'

A FATHER had two sons, one of whom was very bright, and became a professor of mathematics at Glasgow university. The second, younger son, became a cobbler, like his father, as he was considered very dim, and had failed his Standard Grades. The second son eventually became a millionaire, and attributed his success to a piece of advice from his father, 'Be content with small margins on a large turnover'. 'So,' said the millionaire, 'my shoes are made for two pounds a pair, and I sell them for five pounds. I'm very happy with three per cent profit.'

SIGN IN a maternity ward:
　'The first five minutes of life are the most dangerous'
To which someone had added underneath:
　'The last five minutes are pretty dodgy too.'

SIGN ON a bumper sticker heading into Glasgow:
　'I owe, I owe, so off to work I go.'

SIGN IN an Edinburgh jewellers:
　'Ears pierced while you wait.'

A LADY expressed amazement when her daughter allowed her friend to have first go on her new ice skates. 'That's all right mum, I didn't know how thick the ice was.'

A FRIEND told me he wanted a divorce, as his wife kept a pot bellied pig in their bedroom, and the smell was awful. When I suggested he kept the bedroom window open, he said, 'What, and let all my pigeons out?'

TRANQUILLISERS ONLY work if you follow the advice on the bottle: 'Keep away from children'.

A SECRET agent was sent to Ireland to pick up some sensitive photocopies from a local man named Murphy. He had a key phrase to use when he met him, and in a village he asked a farmer if he knew the whereabouts of a man named Murphy. 'You're in luck,' said the farmer. 'Just up the road is the butchers, and his name is Murphy, and the greengrocer's is Murphy's too. Matter of fact my name is Murphy.'
'The grass is green,' says the agent.
'Oh,' says the farmer, 'you want Murphy the spy, he lives over there.'

WHAT I want to know is how do you tell when you've run out of invisible ink?

'GRANDAD, CAN you make a noise like a frog?' 'I think so, but why?' 'Because daddy says he'll be rich when you croak.'

There once was a man on Loch Fyne
Who married three wives at a time
When asked, 'Why a third?'
He replied, 'One's absurd!'
And bigamy, man, is a crime.

Beneath this slab,
Bill Smith is stowed,
He looked at the ads,
And not the road.

Don Brown sent in this joke:

A MAN decided to have a face-lift for his birthday. He spends £5000 and feels really good about the result. On his way home he stops at a news-stand and buys a paper. Before leaving he says to the sales clerk, 'I hope you don't mind me asking, but how old do you think I am?' 'About 35,' is the reply. 'I'm actually 47,' the man says, feeling really good.

After that he goes to McDonald's for lunch, and asks the assistant the same question, to which the reply is, 'Oh you look about 29.' 'I'm actually 47.' This makes him feel really good.

While standing at the bus stop he asks an old woman the same question. She replies, 'I am 85 years old and my eyesight is going. But when I was young there was a sure way of telling a man's age. If I put my hand down your trousers and play with your balls for ten minutes, I will be able to tell your exact age.'

As there was no one around, the man lets her slip her hand down his trousers. Ten minutes later the old lady says, 'OK, it's done. You are 47'.

Stunned, the man says, 'That was brilliant! How did you do that?'

'I was behind you in McDonald's.'

A G Yeardley from Sheffield sent in the next three:

'DAD, WHAT'S the *Kama Sutra*?' asked the ten-year-old lad. 'I'm in trouble now,' thought the dad, but went on to describe in simple words all about it: reasons, methods and positions as far as he could. 'Now do you understand all that son?' 'Yes dad, but one thing puzzles me.' 'Oh what's that son?' asked dad. Came the reply: 'Why did King John have to sign it?'

TWO RADIO presenters are in danger of losing their afternoon show due to falling ratings. They approach their producer with the idea of a phone-in to attract more interest. It would comprise of punters calling in with unusual words or sayings. The producer agrees but tells them that if it doesn't improve the ratings then they're canned. The next day they receive their first caller: 'Hello caller, you're live on air. What's your unusual word?' 'Hello, my unusual word is giurn.'
'Well I've never heard that before. Can you give me an example of how it would be used?' 'Yes,' says the caller, 'Giurn bugger off!'

The producer immediately cuts the call and takes the show off the air. The two presenters plead for another chance claiming that it had been bad luck their plan to rescue the show had failed. The producer agrees to one more try.

The next day they try again, receiving the first call: 'Hello caller, you're live on air. What's your unusual word?' 'Hello, my unusual word is smee.' 'Smee,' says the presenter. 'That really is unusual and how would you use that in a sentence.'
'Smee again, giurn bugger off!'

WHERE DO ghosts like to swim?
In the Dead Sea.

This is from Evelyn Marsden from Culross:

WHAT DID mama-mia see when she looked over the wall?
Papa-Pia.

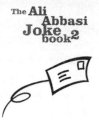

James A Kelly from Wigtownshire sent in the following two jokes:

Scottish Wedding Proposal: You're what?

Hector: 'You said this was a 12-year-old malt.'
Duncan: 'Aye.'
Hector: 'Very small for its age.'

The next three are from Keith T Shanahan from Drains Bay:

HOW CAN you tell golfers' socks?
  There's a hole in one.

IT'S BEEN a Victor Sylvester winter – sleet, sleet, sleet, sleet – snow.

HOW MANY ears has (Vulcan) Mr Spock?
  Three. One left ear, one right ear and one final front ear.

This is from John Harrison from Rosyth:

SON: 'WHERE'S the remote control for the TV?'

Father: 'When I was your age I was the remote control!'

Tim Mickleburgh from Grimsby sent this one in:

A MAGICIAN is walking on a remote moor, he comes across a man looking miserable. To cheer him up he promises the man that he will grant him one wish.

'Really? Well in that case, I'd like to be able to turn soil into gold.'

'Mmmm ... that could be a little difficult. Have you any other desires?'

'Well I always wanted to understand the workings of the female mind.'

'How about the gold?'

Bob Docherty from Essex sent this in:

A FARMER has a large field of hay. His son doesn't want to be a farmer and moves to Glasgow – but the only job that he could find was shining shoes.

Now the farmer makes hay while the son shines!

This was sent in by Mrs M Napier from Dumbarton:

WHAT DID one flea say to the other flea?
    Shall we walk or take a cat!

Mrs S Begg from Stratford-on-Avon sent in this:

HEARD ABOUT the student nurse who was told to give the patient an air-ring?
    She took him out for a walk.

Ian McLaren from Edinburgh sent this in:

A FARMER bought a zebra from a bankrupt circus. One day when walking round the farm the zebra met a bull.
    'What do you do on the farm?' the zebra asked
    The bull replied, 'Take your pyjamas off gorgeous and I'll show you!'

Melissa and Ellyn Burnett from Rothie Norman sent this joke in:

WHY DID the bee fly over the motorway?
    It was looking for a BP station!

Mrs E Harris sent this joke in:

WHAT DID the camera say to the light bulb?
    Hang around, I'll be back in a flash!

This is from William Tyroll from Glasgow:

MY UNCLE was a great collector of clocks, watches, and time pieces all his life. He died and it took two weeks to wind up his estate.

James Steele from Paisley sent this in:

A BOY says to his dad: 'Dad can you give me money to buy a torch?'
    Dad: 'What do you want a torch for?'
    Son: 'So that I can get myself a girlfriend.'
    Dad: 'Listen son, when I was your age I didn't need a torch to get myself a girlfriend.'
    Son: 'I know, and look what you finished up with.'

William Hay-Parker of Sheffield sent the next three jokes in:

A SCOTSMAN lay ill in hospital, and round his bed with three of his best pals.

He said to them all, 'In case anything happens to me, I'd like to leave you all a wee tartan souvenir'

The first pal said, 'Ah widnae mind a wee tartan scarf.'

'Ah'd like your wee tartan kilt,' said the second.

The third said, 'Could ah hae aw yer money, a've got a wee tart in trouble!'

A TOURIST walked into a general store in a village in the Highlands. In front of a big roaring fire stood the owner with his back to the fire and his hands behind him. The tourist looked up at some hams hanging from hooks above the counter ...

'Is that your Ayrshire bacon?' he asked.

'No,' was the answer, 'I'm just warming my hands'

AROUND THE coffin stood an Englishman, an Irishman, and a Scotsman. The Englishman put a five pound note on the coffin and said: 'Wherever you are, have a drink on me Taffy.' The Irishman did likewise. The Scotsman said, 'Aye, hae a drink on me as well,' wrote out a cheque for £15 and took the two five pound notes as change.

N Kerr from Helensburgh sent this joke in:

A RABBIT went into a bar and asked for a cheese toastie and Guinness, which he downed at one. He then asked for a chicken toastie and Guinness and this was also downed. Then his third order, a ham toastie and Guinness – was again swallowed. Then he collapsed. The barman said, 'I thought you were getting them down too fast.' To which the rabbit replied, 'No it was mixin' ma toasties'

Mrs R Evans Llandrillo sent this in:

'BILL HAD a serious eye affliction,' said the specialist, 'everything he looked at he saw double.'
'Poor chap' replied the nurse, 'I suppose he has trouble finding a job?'
'Not at all,' the doctor explained, 'the gas company snapped him up – now he's reading meters'

Mrs B Rudd Whitehaven sent this in:

(DRUNKEN) MAN heckling ventriloquist on stage:
    'You're rubbish, no talent, get off.'
    Dummy answers: 'He's very good and you can't see his lips moving.'
    Man replies: 'You mind your own business. I'm not talking to you.'

Rachel Mangto (age 9) from Dalgety Bay, sent the next three jokes in:

WHAT DID the horse say to his friend the pig?
　　Hello Neighbour.

WHY WAS the bear cold?
　　Because he was bare.

WHAT KIND of smile does a mouse have?
　　A cheesy smile.

This is from Mrs J Singer in Leeds:

A MAN walks into a pub and orders a double whisky, telling the barmaid: 'I shouldn't be drinking this with what I've got.'
　　'What's that?' she enquires.
　　'Fifty pence!' he replies.

This is from S Rattray, Glasgow:

THERE WERE two crisps walking along a road when a car stopped and asked them if they wanted a lift – the crisps replied, 'No thanks, we're walkers.'

Mrs Gladys Dalton from Sheffield sent this in:

A MOUSE went into a music shop for a mouth organ. The assistant said:

'That's unusual, we had another mouse come in for one this morning.'

The mouse replied, 'Oh, that would be our Monica.'

Mr Alan Pon from Hawick sent this in:

A SMALL boy was going to his posh aunt's. His mother warned him beforehand, 'Don't say I want to go to the toilet – that's rude – say I want to whisper instead'. Anyway off they went to the Grande Dame. Sure enough, wee Johnny, half way through the meal piped up, 'I want to whisper.'

'That's alright,' the posh aunt said, 'you can whisper in my ear.'

Mrs J Hall from Alford in Aberdeenshire sent this final joke:

A WIFE sent her husband to her local market to buy a duck for their Christmas dinner. Before leaving he donned a pair of overalls to do some odd jobs about the place. He left and caught the bus to market and wandered round the stalls until he found what he wanted. Unfortunately it was still alive and the only one left. The seller assured him it was a very quiet and tame duck and would be no problem to take home on the bus.

As he had an hour or so to spare he decided to pass the time at the local picture house, but he was told that no animals were allowed in. So he went out round the corner and put the duck down his overalls and went back. He got a seat next to two elderly ladies who were enjoying the film with their sweets and crisps. The duck behaved impeccably having fallen asleep in the warmth and dark, but inevitably it began to move around as it got warmer and searched for an outlet to get some air.

Meanwhile the lady sitting next to him whispered urgently to her friend that she thought they should move to another row of seats. Her companion was quite comfortable and asked why she wanted to move. Her friend informed her in a state of alarm that the man next to her was 'one of those' and 'showing his you know what'. Her companion replied, 'Ach, I ken that,'

'Bit nae ane like this,' said her friend.

'What's it like then?' asked her friend, 'see ane, see them aw.'

'Na, bit this ane's eatin' my crisps.'